FARM DAY

Written by Sarah Tatler

Illustrated by Laura Cornell

 ScottForesman

A Division of HarperCollins*Publishers*

On the farm. . .

we can see a pig.

We can pet a cow.

We can hear a rooster.

We can smell some flowers.

6

We can eat some corn.

7

We can play in the hay!
Oh, yay!